MASTERING THE ART OF FRUGALITY:

A Comprehensive Guide to Saving Money and Building Wealth

FRED CASOM

Disclaimer:

This guide's content is for educational purposes only, and it shouldn't be construed as financial advice. The techniques and advice included in this manual may not be appropriate for everyone and should be customised to your unique financial position and goals. Seek the counsel of a certified financial adviser before making any financial decisions. Any losses, damages, or other liabilities sustained as a result of using the advice provided in this guide are not the responsibility of the guide's author or publisher. Before making any investments or financial decisions, the reader should do their own research and due diligence and bear all responsibility for any decisions.

Copyright @2022 by Fred casom

All rights Reserved
No part of this publication may be reproduced, distributed, or transmitted in any form by any means, including photocopying, recording, or other electronic or mechanical method, or by any information storage and retrieval system without the prior written permission of the publisher, except in the case of very brief quotation embodied in critical review.

TABLE OF CONTENTS

CHAPTER ONE:
The Psychology of Spending: Understanding Why We Overspend and How to Overcome It   6

CHAPTER TWO:
Creating a Budget That Works: Setting Realistic Goals and Sticking to Them   10

CHAPTER THREE:
Cutting Costs without Sacrificing Quality: Tips for Saving on Everyday Expenses   14

CHAPTER FOUR:
Maximising Your Income: Strategies for Earning More Money and Increasing Your Savings   18

CHAPTER FIVE:
Investing in Your Future: Building Wealth Through Smart Saving and Investing Habits   22

CHAPTER SIX:
Staying Motivated: Finding Inspiration and Accountability to Stay on Track with Your Financial Goals   27

Conclusion   32

CHAPTER ONE:
The Psychology of Spending: Understanding Why We Overspend and How to Overcome It

Understanding our spending tendencies is a crucial first step in improving our money management. The feelings we experience, such as tension, anxiety, or even boredom, frequently influence the way we spend our money. Shopping and other forms of spending can be used as a coping mechanism for difficult feelings or as a method to congratulate ourselves for a job well done. These behaviours can, however, easily deteriorate into unhealthy ones and cause monetary pressure. Self-awareness and the ability to identify the underlying emotional triggers that cause our expenditure are crucial for overcoming excess. We may start to end the pattern of overspending and develop better money management skills by learning to identify and control these triggers.

Our purchasing patterns might be influenced by social and cultural factors in addition to emotional causes. For instance, we could experience pressure to live up to society norms or to stay up with our peers' standards of life. It may be challenging to prioritise our financial goals and maintain control over our expenditure due to these outside factors. It's important to keep in mind, though, that material things or outside approval are not the only factors that define financial success.

We can take charge of our finances and strive toward a more meaningful and sustainable future by learning to put our own values and aspirations first.

Recognizing how advertising and marketing influence our purchasing behaviour is crucial to understanding our spending patterns. Advertisers employ a variety of strategies to instil a sense of urgency or desire in us, which frequently prompts us to make impulsive or pointless purchases. We can learn to make more informed and deliberate purchasing decisions by raising our awareness of these strategies. To help us keep on track with our financial goals, we can also look for alternate sources of knowledge and assistance, including financial advisors or neighbourhood organisations. In the end, understanding the psychology of spending needs a combination of introspection, education, and support, but it can eventually result in considerable gains in our financial welfare.

Understanding that being frugal doesn't only entail being cheap or depriving ourselves of the things we enjoy is essential if we want to genuinely master the art of being thrifty. Instead, the focus should be on striking a balance and staying within our means while yet reaching our financial objectives. This requires us to change our perspective and adopt a long-term outlook, putting more emphasis on the advantages of saving money than the trade-offs we must make in the short term. For instance, we can contribute more to our emergency fund or retirement by spending less on necessities like groceries and leisure. We can make little but significant improvements that build up over time by recognizing the true value of our money and the impact of compound interest. Finding a sense of fulfilment in our financial decisions rather than just pursuing fleeting pleasures or status symbols is ultimately the goal of mastering the psychology of spending.

Making a spending plan or budget is a useful method for preventing overspending. This entails taking a sincere look at our income and costs and establishing reasonable spending targets for each category. We may make more purposeful and thoughtful financial decisions by establishing clear boundaries and priorities. Remember that budgeting doesn't have to be constructive or constrained; rather, it may be a tool for achieving more control and freedom over our finances. Keeping tabs on our expenditures and constantly evaluating our budget can also help us maintain accountability and make necessary adjustments. We can create healthy habits that promote our overall wellness by remaining committed to our long-term financial goals and coordinating our spending with our ideals.

CHAPTER TWO:
Creating a Budget That Works: Setting Realistic Goals and Sticking to Them

In order to perfect the art of frugality, creating a budget can be a difficult process. A successful budget should take into consideration both fixed and variable spending and be customised to our individual financial status and goals. Gathering all of our financial records and making an extensive list of our income and expenses before we begin is beneficial. Expenses including rent or mortgage, energy bills, auto payments, groceries, entertainment, and savings contributions may be considered. We can start allocating our funds to various categories once we have a thorough understanding of our financial status, taking into account our priorities and aspirations. Because unforeseen expenses or changes in income can happen at any time, it's critical to be flexible and practical while creating a budget. To assess our progress and make any necessary adjustments, we should also routinely review our budget. We can attain our long-term objectives and establish more financial security by making a budget that works for us and adhering to it over time.

Setting realistic objectives for ourselves is one of the most important aspects of making a successful budget. This entails considering both our long-term financial objectives and our current income and expenses. For instance, if our objective is to save for a down payment on a house, we might need to limit our discretionary spending to make more room for savings. To avoid frustration or burnout, it's crucial to balance our short- and long-term objectives. We should also avoid having too high of expectations. To further assist us in staying on track and avoiding overspending, we can set up automated savings contributions or use budgeting applications. We can establish sound financial practices that contribute to our general welfare by defining attainable goals and making a budget that suits our particular needs.

Learning to prioritise our expenditures based on our beliefs and goals is a crucial component of effective budgeting. This necessitates a closer examination of our spending to distinguish between what is actually necessary and what is more optional. For instance, even if we might need to pay for housing and utilities, we could be able to reduce spending on entertainment or eat out to save more money. In addition, we should be aware of our spending patterns and refrain from impulsive or pointless purchases that can derail our finances. We may increase our financial security and live within our means by making deliberate, informed decisions about our spending.

Anticipating and making plans for irregular or unforeseen spending is another useful technique for making a budget that works. These could involve items like auto repairs, hospital bills, or vacation costs. We may prevent the stress and financial hardship that can result from unforeseen charges by allocating a portion of our budget for these kinds of expenses. In order to prevent overspending in particular areas, we should also be aware of our spending habits and change our budget as necessary. For instance, if we routinely spend more on groceries than we planned, we may need to reevaluate our grocery budget or look for methods to reduce wasteful spending in other areas. We can eventually reach better financial stability and success by maintaining flexibility and adaptability in our budgeting strategy.

Finding strategies to boost our revenue and save costs is a last component of a successful budget. To do this, we might need to haggle for a pay increase at work, take on a side job or freelance employment, or look for methods to lower our monthly expenses. For instance, we might be able to switch to a more affordable phone plan, reduce our subscription services, or figure out how to reduce our home energy bills. We can also think of original ways to make extra money, like starting a small business or selling unneeded stuff. We can have more money to invest toward our long-term financial goals and increase our financial security by raising our income and lowering our spending.

CHAPTER THREE:
Cutting Costs without Sacrificing Quality: Tips for Saving on Everyday Expenses

The next step after creating a budget and learning to live within our means is to find ways to increase our savings and reduce expenses wherever we can. This might entail looking more closely at our ongoing costs and identifying strategies to cut them back on them or do away with them entirely. For instance, we may look into refinancing our car or house loan to get a cheaper interest rate, or we could bargain with our insurance company to get our premiums reduced. Additionally, there are strategies to reduce discretionary expenditure, such as cooking more meals at home, using coupons and discount codes, or purchasing pre-owned things rather than brand-new ones. These minor changes to our spending patterns can help us save a lot more money over time and get closer to our financial objectives.

Utilising the rewards and loyalty programs provided by stores, credit card providers, and other organisations is another efficient approach to increase our savings. We can acquire cashback, discounts, and other rewards by enrolling in these programs and making regular use of them, and these rewards can accumulate over time. We can also explore additional revenue streams like reward programs, cashback applications, and online surveys. These little but regular sources of income can add up quickly and hasten the completion of our financial objectives. We may make the most of our expenditure and increase our savings by being strategic about the programs we take part in and optimising our rewards and incentives.

Utilising tax-advantaged accounts and investment options is another smart way to increase our savings. Contributions to 401(k) or IRA accounts, which may offer tax advantages and compound interest over time, may be included in this. We may also think about investing in securities like stocks, bonds, or real estate, which have the potential to generate steady returns over the long term and increase wealth. However, because the market can be erratic and risky, it's crucial to conduct due diligence and speak with a financial expert before making any significant investments. We may gradually build our wealth and ensure our financial future by investing with a long-term perspective.

Finally, it's crucial to keep a frugal and uncomplicated mindset in order to optimise our savings and gradually accumulate riches. In addition to finding delight in more straightforward things like spending time with loved ones, taking in the scenery, or engaging in creative activities, this may entail practising mindful consumption and avoiding pointless expenditures. We can increase our sense of fulfilment and happiness while simultaneously achieving our financial goals by concentrating on the things that are most important to us and living within our means. We can also discover ways to give back to our communities and to the issues we care about, which can offer us a sense of fulfilment and purpose that goes beyond financial goods. We may optimise our savings and live a more purposeful and fulfilled life by practising an attitude of thankfulness and simplicity.

It's also critical to be aware of cognitive biases and how they may affect how much and how little we spend and save. For instance, when we're stressed or concerned, we could be more prone to buy something on impulse, or we might be tempted to overspend when we observe other people doing it. We can improve the quality of our financial judgments by identifying these biases and taking actions to reduce them. Setting specific financial objectives, keeping tabs on our spending patterns, and asking dependable friends or family members to hold us accountable may all be part of this. In order to make decisions that are in line with our values and long-term financial goals, we can also practise self-awareness and mindfulness with regard to our spending patterns.

CHAPTER FOUR:
Maximising Your Income: Strategies for Earning More Money and Increasing Your Savings

To reach your financial objectives and enhance your entire financial status, you must maximise your income. Here are some methods for growing your income and your savings:

1. Improve Your Earning Potential:
 Improving your earning potential is the first step to optimising your income. This can be achieved by learning new skills, completing further coursework or certification, connecting with industry experts, and taking on more responsibility at work.

2. Search for fresh opportunities :
Keep an eye out for better-paying career prospects. For job openings, search online job boards, company websites, and professional groups in your industry.

3. Start a Side Business :
You can utilise the additional income from a side job to reduce debt or build up your savings. Think about beginning a freelance business, an internet store, or offering a service you are good at.

4. Discuss Your Salary:
Consider negotiating your wage with your company if you believe you are not being paid what you are worth. Do your homework and support your request

with evidence of your efforts and professional successes.

5. Cut Your Expenses:
You can save more money each month if you reduce your costs. Find ways to cut back on your spending in areas like entertainment, eating out, or transportation.

6. Establish a Budget:
You may track your expenditure and find areas for cost-cutting by making a budget. Spend a portion of your salary on things like housing, food, transportation, and savings.

7. Automatically Save:
Make monthly transfers from your checking account to your savings account so they happen automatically. You can do this without even realising it to save money.

8. Invest in your future:
You can gradually increase your wealth by making investments in stocks, mutual funds, or real estate. To uncover the greatest investing opportunities for you, speak with a financial professional or conduct your own study.

9. Leverage Your Assets:
If you want to make more money, think about using your assets, such as your house or automobile.

Use your automobile for ride-sharing services or consider renting out a spare room.

10. Use Tax Breaks to Your Advantage:
Make sure you are utilising all accessible tax benefits to lower your tax obligation and boost your income. To assist you in locating allowable deductions, get advice from a tax expert or use tax software.

11. Think about a Career Change:
Consider changing your career if you are dissatisfied with your present employment or earning potential. Look for sectors where there is a rising need for competent personnel and growth.

12. Build Your Network:
You can meet new clients or investors, locate new career prospects, and gain knowledge from other experts in your sector by networking. Attend industry conferences, sign up for trade organisations, and establish LinkedIn connections.

You may improve your savings and maximise your income by putting these techniques into practice. Always be patient and set reasonable goals because accumulating wealth requires time and work. You can achieve financial freedom and build a brighter future for yourself and your loved ones by making little daily progresses.

CHAPTER FIVE:
Investing in Your Future: Building Wealth Through Smart Saving and Investing Habits

Building long-term wealth and establishing financial security require you to make significant investments in your future. It entails forming wise spending and investing practices that support the long-term growth of your assets. Discipline, perseverance, and a desire to learn about various investment possibilities and strategies are necessary to build wealth through investing. You can take advantage of compound interest and experience exponential wealth growth by making early and regular investments. To minimise risk and optimise rewards, it's crucial to diversify your investing portfolio. To make wise investment choices, whether you decide to invest in stocks, bonds, real estate, or other asset classes, it is crucial to speak with a financial advisor or conduct your own study. You may create a strong financial foundation that supports your long-term objectives and aspirations with a sound savings and investing strategy.

As part of your wealth-building strategy, it's critical to handle debt responsibly in addition to saving money and making investments. Credit card debt, for example, eats up your savings quickly and restricts your ability to invest. You may keep moving toward your financial objectives by prioritising debt repayment and avoiding high-interest debt whenever you can. Having an emergency fund is essential for protecting your investments during periods of market volatility as well as for paying for unforeseen needs. You can accumulate wealth and reach financial independence over time by cultivating sound money management techniques and adhering to a long-term investment and savings plan. Keep in mind that creating wealth takes time and demands dedication and persistent effort. You may create a stable financial future for yourself and your loved ones by exercising patience, perseverance, and a willingness to learn and adapt.

Managing your emotions is a crucial component of accumulating wealth through wise saving and investment practices. Investors may experience anxiety or greed as a result of the volatility and short-term fluctuations that might occur in the investment markets. Avoid making snap judgments based on feelings, and keep your eyes on your long-term investment objectives. Risk can be reduced and returns can be more stable over time with a well-diversified investment portfolio that combines a variety of various asset classes and investing strategies. Additionally, it's crucial to frequently examine and modify your investment strategy to keep it in line with your shifting objectives and risk tolerance. You may create a strong investing portfolio that supports your long-term financial goals by remaining focused, disciplined, and knowledgeable.

Adopting a thrifty lifestyle and limiting unnecessary spending are further components of creating money through wise saving and investment practices. You can cut back on your spending and have more money for savings and investments by putting more emphasis on your needs than your wants. You can save a lot of money over time by making small lifestyle adjustments like cooking at home instead of eating out, using the bus or train instead of driving a car, or purchasing used goods instead of brand-new ones. Your earning potential and long-term wealth can both be increased by investing in yourself, such as through schooling or learning new skills. You may create a solid financial foundation that supports your objectives and aspirations by making good financial decisions and living within your means.

When accumulating wealth through wise saving and investing practices, it is crucial to have a clear grasp of your financial goals and priorities. Setting clear, attainable financial objectives is required, such as setting aside money for a down payment on a home, paying off debt, or preparing for retirement. You can maintain motivation and focus on your long-term financial ambitions by breaking your goals down into smaller, doable steps. To make sure you are on track to achieve your goals, it is also crucial to monitor your progress and make any necessary adjustments to your savings and investment plan. You can attain financial independence and live in safety and comfort by developing sound financial practices and remaining devoted to your goals. Building wealth is a long-term process that calls for patience, tenacity, and discipline.

CHAPTER SIX:
Staying Motivated: Finding Inspiration and Accountability to Stay on Track with Your Financial Goals

Maintaining motivation is crucial when pursuing your financial objectives. When there are conflicting priorities, unforeseen expenses, or market volatility, it is simple to become demotivated or distracted. However, you can stay on track and meet your financial goals by finding inspiration and accountability. Visualising the advantages of reaching your financial goals, such as financial freedom, stability, and peace of mind, might help you stay motivated. By focusing on the greater picture instead of passing distractions, you can maintain your attentionFinding an accountability partner, such as a dependable friend, relative, or financial advisor, who can offer advice, support, and feedback as you work toward your goals, is another tactic. Additionally, you can stay motivated and keep moving forward by keeping track of your progress, acknowledging small victories, and learning from failures. Achieving long-term financial success requires keeping motivated because accumulating wealth is a journey rather than a destination.

Joining a group of like-minded people who are pursuing comparable financial objectives is another approach to maintain motivation and accountability. This can take the form of a neighbourhood financial organisation or an online community like a social media group or personal finance blog. When pursuing your financial objectives, these communities can offer a sense of support, motivation, and accountability that can be invaluable. You can learn from others' experiences, open your mind to new ideas, and maintain your progress toward reaching your financial objectives by sharing your triumphs, setbacks, and insights with others. You can also keep motivated and focused on your long-term goals by finding inspiration in personal finance books, podcasts, or financial success stories. You may reach your financial goals and live a more secure and meaningful life by being motivated and responsible. Building wealth is a marathon, not a sprint.

It's crucial to understand that maintaining motivation involves both appreciating the process of achieving financial success and concentrating on the goal at hand. You can stay motivated and avoid burnout by setting minor goals along the way and acknowledging your accomplishments. This can involve setting up and adhering to a budget, eliminating debt, or making steady progress toward your retirement savings objectives. You may maintain your motivation and have fun on the road to financial freedom by acknowledging tiny victories along the route. It's crucial to keep in mind that failures and difficulties are a normal part of the path to financial success. It's crucial to learn from these failures and utilise them as chances to expand and enhance your financial strategy rather than becoming disheartened or quitting up. You can overcome any challenge and accomplish your long-term financial objectives by remaining adaptable, strong, and driven.

A mentality change is necessary to keep motivated and accountable to your financial goals. This entails having a growth mentality and being willing to experiment, learn, and adapt. There is no one-size-fits-all method for accumulating wealth, so what works for one person might not work for another. You may improve your financial strategy and have more success if you're open to new concepts, tactics, and chances. Additionally, maintaining motivation necessitates having a positive outlook, being open to new experiences, and being willing to take calculated risks. This can entail making an investment in your future, launching a new company, or seeking a job shift that is in line with your financial objectives. You can stay motivated, be held accountable, and reach your long-term financial goals by approaching your financial journey with a growth mentality and a positive attitude.

Having a firm knowledge of your beliefs and priorities is crucial for maintaining motivation. Your financial path can have more meaning and purpose if your financial objectives are in line with your personal values. If helping others in your community is essential to you, for instance, you can decide to incorporate charity giving into your financial plan. Similar to how you would prioritise saving for a family vacation or other shared activities if spending time with family and friends is a priority. You may maintain motivation and a sense of purpose by connecting your financial goals with your personal beliefs, which will make it easier for you to stick with your long-term financial goals.

CONCLUSION

In conclusion, developing the art of frugality is a key component of creating money and succeeding financially. You can live a more contented and financially secure life by developing a thrifty attitude, setting spending priorities, and improving your saving and investment behaviours. Frugality is not about denying yourself enjoyment or limiting the things you enjoy; rather, it is about striking a balance between your spending and saving behaviours in order to improve your financial situation. The techniques and advice in this manual can help you reach your financial objectives and create lasting wealth, regardless of where you are in your financial journey or whether you want to maximise your current financial plan. You may master the art of frugality and lead a more financially secure and rewarding life by making deliberate decisions, exercising discipline, and adopting a growth mindset.

It's crucial to remember that perfecting the art of frugality requires ongoing learning, experimenting, and development rather than a single effort. Your frugality tactics might need to be modified as your priorities and financial condition change. To improve your financial well-being, it's critical to be adaptable, impartial, and eager to try new things. Don't forget to recognize your accomplishments as you go along. You may maintain motivation and continue to move forward with your financial goals by recognizing and celebrating your financial victories, no matter how big or small. Keep in mind that every modest move you take will help you succeed financially and accumulate wealth over the long term.

Developing the art of frugality involves more than just increasing one's riches; it also involves having a beneficial influence on society and the environment. You may help create a more equitable and sustainable society by consuming less and giving priority to sustainable and ethical goods and services. Additionally, by being frugal, you can encourage others to follow suit, bringing about positive change both within and outside of your community. So learning to be frugal can help you succeed financially as well as contribute to a world that is more fair, just, and sustainable.

The art of frugality involves deliberate choices that enhance your financial health and are consistent with your values and priorities, rather than simply being thrifty in terms of money. You may reach your financial objectives and amass long-term wealth by adopting a thrifty attitude, prioritising your spending, maximising your saving and investing behaviours, and remaining adaptable and flexible. Furthermore, being frugal can have a positive influence on society and the environment, encouraging others to follow suit and causing a positive chain reaction. Frugality is about striking a balance between your spending and saving habits to live a more meaningful and secure life, not about making sacrifices or depriving yourself. You may master the art of being frugal and take pleasure in a more just and sustainable future if you have the correct attitude and techniques.

www.ingramcontent.com/pod-product-compliance
Lightning Source LLC
Chambersburg PA
CBHW031514210526
45464CB00007B/2906